your journey has meaning

Dream….Keep It Moving

Living your
Dreams
is not what happens to
you
It's what you do
with what happens to
you
that makes you live your
Dreams

Quotes are taken from Google and do not directly promote the book

Cynthiawalker1976@gmail.com

Additional copies can be requested by emailing

Cynthiawalker1976@gmail.com

Subject title 'Dream Orders'

Copyright © 2015 Cynthia Walker

Cover page designed by William Walker

Edits done by Heather Walker

All rights reserved.

ISBN:10:151509748X
ISBN-13:978-1515097488

DEDICATION

I dedicate this book to every young lady that needed to hear the words I love you from time to time. To every young lady that needed to hear good job or I'm proud of you every so often. I love you and I'm proud of you. I wrote this book to tell you that you are a survivor because God has destined you to survive. You are already a winner because God has already said you won. I encourage you to keep dreaming and keep it moving, your greater is around the corner.

I love you and I'm proud of you!!!!!!!!!!

Cynthia Walker

To my children Javonta, DeMarcis and Laciona, I love you guys with every ounce of my soul. I thank you for loving me and supporting me. I had you guys so young and didn't always do things right. Even though I am mom and we grew up together, that may have been tough at times so for that I apologize and for anything that you may of missed out on in life.

To my spiritual mother and the ladies of the Friday night book club: You guys have supported me through a tough transition in my life. You have loved me, encouraged me, and pushed me to not only unleash who I am but also what I am. I stand proud to say that I am a saved woman of God. Thank you guys for allowing God to work through you to work on me. Project "Tore up from the floor up" is complete and I'm off and running.

Dream: A Subconscious view of what God has designated for your life.

Keep It Moving: Take what was taught to you and make it so powerful that you too become a legend

CONTENTS

Bonus Pages:
You have to Dream to Dream
I Can Dream
I Will Dream
I Must Dream

ACKNOWLEDGMENTS

I would like to thank three special people that helped and pushed me along the way on this project:

Tamela Brown (The Teacher) Thank you for your input and guidance in making this a learning tool. Your belief in me and this project means the world to me.

Damon Arnold (The Sergeant) Thank you for applying the pressure. Every time I seen you I knew I would have to report in on my progress and give you a date for completion. The first thing you would say to me is 'How is Dream Doing'?

Chris Sain (The Genius) Football made our paths cross only to lead us into a partnership that is not only impacting our community but also changing the world. You are an inspirational 'Big/Little' brother that I will continuously strive to keep up with and make proud. Thank you.

Dear Reader,

You are about to go on a journey with Dream through her healing. Dream is a young lady that is exposing some things about her life that none of her peers know about her. I hope that you won't judge her but that you will open your hearts and minds to see her life from her shoes. If you find some of the aspects of Dream's life similar to yours or you have things you feel like you need to get out I encourage you to journal your thoughts on the pages provided in this book. Now prepare yourselves to enter into the beginning of an experience that you will never forget. Always remember to dream and keep it moving.

I love you…..Cynthia Walker

1 MY NAME IS DREAM

I'm lying in my bed staring at the ceiling mad as

hell

Silently yelling does anyone want to hear the story

I have to tell

Let me introduce myself my name is Dream and

I'm one of four

We were all born to a selfish money hungry whore

When things are slow we eat ravioli out of a can

Steak and potatoes when she lucky enough to find

a man

My siblings and I used to enjoy watching Law and

Order you know staying up late

This dude been here 2 weeks and now the rule is

all kids in bed by 8

She likes to cater to these men she brags treat

them like a king

After all her hard work she always come up empty

not even a ring

Yes no ring and nothing else to show

Nothing but the test results that say yes you are a

hoe

These men only fool with my mommy for a place

to stay

When she start getting clingy they pack up and be

on their way

She don't bother with us when she got a boo

Mommy help me with my homework girl you betta

do what you do

That's what she say to me so I go to my room and

cry

I wish I had a lot of money maybe then some of

her time I could buy

So tired of always feeling so alone

Mommy has no time for me and my daddy I have

never really known

Every night I pray to God please find me a new

home

Dear God,

Today was a rough day. I feel like I'm angry all the time. I want my mommy to find love and be happy so our family will be happy. I don't like it when she bring a new guy home and everything in our house changes. God can you help us? Do you even hear me? I will keep talking to you until you answer me.

Yours truly,

DREAM

For every minute you are angry you lose
60 seconds of happiness

Ralph Waldo Emerson

Dream…..Keep It Moving

Write your sad times in sand, write your
good times in stone

George Bernard Shaw

Name 3 things that make you angry. After each one describe how you handled yourself. Was your actions correct or incorrect?

If you could say anything to Dream what would you say?

What type of person do you think Dream is now that you have met her?

Extension Activity

Write a letter to the last person that made you angry or sad.

Dear _____:

Extension Activity

Write a letter for help. What would you like help with in your life?

Dear_____:

Motivation Statement

My name is _____. I

am in control of (enter an

emotion)_____. When I

feel (enter the same

emotion)_____

_____ I will say the following:

I CAN WIN!!!

I WILL WIN!!!

I ALREADY WON!!!

Dream

From myself to myself

2 DREAMER

Every morning I wake I pray God make me a

princess today

I want to be beautiful with some nice clothes so

the kids at school won't have nothing to say

I don't hear no noise I guess my mommy not

going to work again

That's what happen when she drank all night and

live a life of sin

I see a car in the driveway this one must of

stayed the night

Forget about me God can you please just help

Mommy get right

Find her a man that loves her like you do

Find her a man that will love me and my siblings

too

I asked her one day why did she name me

Dream

Because I was unique and beautiful it would

seem

She said meeting my dad was such a nightmare

she needed something to make her smile when

she looked at me so his dirty rotten self wasn't

the only thing she see

She said he was shysty, a thief and never played

his part

I don't know or care about all that all I know is

he is in my heart

He helped create me just like she did

This is too much pressure on me I'm just a kid

Dear God,

I hate my clothes. Girls at school wear nice clothes and they talk about me. Can you give my mommy a lot of money to buy me some nice stuff so the girls at school will like me? There are too many things in my head I just want them to go away. I'm a kid I'm not supposed to worry about this kind of stuff. Do you hear me God? Can you help me? I will keep talking to you until you answer me back

Yours Truly,

DREAM

Every child is a different kind of flower and all

together makes this world a beautiful garden

Unknown

Dream…..Keep It Moving

Wanting to be someone else is a waste of the

person that you are

Marilyn Monroe

What does Dream's story make you feel?

What is something that you gave up on? What

made you give up?

Is there anything that you would change about

your life? If so why?

Extension Activity

Write a letter to your mom

Dear Mom:

Extension Activity

Write a letter to your dad

Dear Dad:

Extension Activity

Write a letter to God

Dear God:

Motivation Statement

Beauty starts on the inside and shines through the

outside. It does not matter what other's opinions

are of me I know I am beautiful!!!!!!!!

Dream

From myself to myself

3 DREAMING

Today I began to imagine who my daddy could be

Is he short and stubby or is he tall as a tree

I must look like him because I don't think I look

like her

My memories of him are little to none just one big

blur

I picture my daddy to mighty and strong too

When I finally find my daddy we will be tighter

than paper and glue

When I find him he is going to rescue me from

this mess

He is waiting for me to find him I guess???????????

He has to be, I long for him so he has to long for

me

I am his daughter one beating heart one in the

same what else could it be??????

Does my daddy even care to be in my life?

Has he threw me away because of him and my

mommy's strife

Lord please put me in his heart

Make him think about me every day this would be

a start

Make him realize that in my life he should play an

important part

Show him what a man and a father should be

Make him seek you God then he would seek me

Lord touch my daddy and my mommy too

Lord touch them both make them brand new

It is never too late for them to get it right open

their eyes Lord make them see the light

God please help me with my family

God please help me with me…………

Dear God,

Why doesn't my daddy love me? What did I do to him? Can you make him come get me? I don't want to live with my mommy any more. She is mean and always yelling at us. God can you hear me? Can you help me? I will keep talking to you until you answer me

Yours truly,

DREAM

Never lose hope you never know what

tomorrow may bring

Unknown

Dream…..Keep It Moving

To conquer frustration one must remain

intensely focused on the outcome not the

obstacles

T.F. Hodge

How does Dream's story about her dad make you

feel?

Who or what has disappointed you in your life?

Explain

How are you like Dream?

How are you different than Dream?

Extension Activities

Write a letter to someone that you have questions

for. In your letter ask your questions and express

how you feel about them.

Motivation Statement

I love myself, I believe in myself. There is nothing that I can fail at. I may have to try again but I will never fail.

Dream

From myself to myself

4 WHY DREAM?

Today is the first day of school but I'm not excited

to go

I have some new stories to tell but no new clothes

to show

Once again my mommy said she has no money I

have to wait

School starts the same time every year why is she

always late

When can I just be a normal kid?

I wish someone would look inside to see all the

things that I've hid

I wish someone would help or just listen to me

I wish someone would look deep into my eyes and

see

The pain, the anger, and all the shame

I can't talk to my parents they are the ones to

blame

I heard this girl in class say she got her North Face

free, she didn't have to pay a dime

And because she didn't get caught it is not

considered a crime

My mommy says you will get nowhere if you lie,

cheat, or steal

Besides God don't like it how do she think He

would feel

I'm too scared to do anything that would send me

to jail

I'm even more scared of things that would send

me to hell

Although I do need a jacket and hers do look nice

Free sounds good especially since I can't play full

price

I think I could do it without getting caught

Besides that would be one less thing that needs to

be bought

At this point I need to do what I need to do

I'm tired of always looking raggedy and through

If I can pull this off maybe I will go back and get

some more

Now just to figure out how to get to the

store……………..

Dear God,

Please don't be mad at me I really need some new clothes. I only plan on taking a few things to help my mommy out you know she don't have the money. If I do this God the girls at my school will stop talking about me and want to be my friend. God are you listening to me? Oh well I tried to talk to you about it before I did it.

Yours truly,

Dream

Don't change to fit the fashion change the fashion to fit you.

Inescable Beauty

Dream…..Keep It Moving

Why fit in when you were born to stand out

Dr. Seuss

Have you ever experienced peer pressure? How did you handle it?

What has been the hardest thing that you ever dealt with at school?

Have you ever been in a situation where you were about to do something you knew was wrong? Explain

Do you feel like you have anyone at your school that you can talk to about personal issues? Please explain your answer

What things do you need someone to talk to about?

Extension Activity

With what you know about Dream so far create a conversation with her below:

Me:

Dream:

Me:

Dream:

Me:

Dream:

Me:

Dream:

Use additional sheets of paper if needed.

Extension Activity

Instructions: Using magazines create Dream a dream outfit from head to feet on this page. Describe your choices.

Motivation Statement:

My name is _____. I am not defined by the brand names on my clothes. I am defined by the brand I create myself to be. I am fearfully, wonderfully and uniquely made to be GREAT!!!!!!

Dream

From myself To myself

5 DO DREAMS COME TRUE?

I woke up this morning smiling about my dream

from the night before

My bedroom was huge with a big bed and clothes

galore

I couldn't decide what to wear so I called in the

maid to chose

I had to rush to get ready because I had slept

through my snooze

Once I was dressed I ran outside to get in my car

drop top, shades on I was looking like a star

DREAM WAKE UP AND GET OUT THAT

BED!!!!!!!!!!!!

GET DOWN TO THIS KITCHEN OR YOU ARE NOT GETTING FED!!!!!!!!

What a way to spoil a perfect dream

Why does that woman always have to be so mean?

I don't need a maid to help me pick out what I

wore the day before

God I just want to stay home I don't even want to

open this door

If I don't she will come yelling again and again

Do dreams ever come true? Will I ever win?

Good morning she says with a smile on her face

your birthday is on its way

She asked how I wanted to celebrate my big day

Every year I tell her and every year she lets me

down

Every birthday I get up with a smile and lay down

with a frown

I told her this year I want to spend the whole day

with just us two

Lunch, shopping maybe even a new hair do

She smiled and said ok she will plan everything out

I was excited at first but then came the doubt

That it will even happen this year like all the other

Do dreams ever come true? Not with this mother

Happy birthday to me…….

Dear God,

Why can't my life be a dream? All I want is a birthday where I can feel special. Every year all I get is a cake and broken promises. I know my mom tries but why can't my family have money to do special things. I see that my mommy works a lot and she never has any money to do special things with us. God can you hear me? I will keep talking to you until you answer me back.

Yours truly,

Dream

Your parents may not be perfect but they are the most perfect gift God has ever given you

Unknown

Dream…..Keep It Moving

Manage your expectations and you'll manage your disappointments

Todd Lohenry

Have you ever been let down? How did you feel?
Did you share your feelings with the person or
people that let you down?

Write about your favorite birthday. Why was it your favorite?

Extension Activity

Find 3 of your peers and ask them to describe the biggest disappointment the experienced in their life and how they dealt with it. Write one page about what you learned. How does their experience compare to your disappointments. (Additional page available)

Extension Activity cont.

Motivation Statement:

My Happiness outweighs sadness, my joy

outweighs my disappointment, my dreams

outweigh my reality. I will continue to move

forward.

Dream

From myself to myself

6 DAY DREAM

I dragged my feet walking home from the bus stop

today

Not excited to go home I actually thought about

running away

But to my surprise as I opened the front door

I saw presents marked Dream, I counted at least

four

Could it be, it just might be, that God has

answered my prayers

I asked him to make this the best birthday for me

I began to cry so hard I could not see

As I wiped my eyes my mom and dad appeared

and yelled HAPPY BIRTHDAY DREAM!!!!!!!

We wanted to surprise you and show you that we

can work as a team

We wanted to make this the best birthday you ever

had

From this birthday on we promise you will never

have one that will be sad

We are sorry for anytime that we let you down

We are sorry for anytime you had to wear a frown

Dream you are a beautiful princess that deserves to

wear a crown

Go get dressed baby girl we are taking you out on

the town

At that moment I heard a loud bell

At that moment I jumped up and then fell

At that moment my teacher said Dream don't ever

fall asleep in my class

But since it is your birthday this time I will give

you a pass

Dear God,

I give up ever expecting to have a happy birthday.

No one cares about me what is the point of having

a birthday? Why does my life have to be so

complicated? I wish my birthday to be about me,

presents, cake, family, and a lot of fun. God can

you make my birthday wish come true? God do

you hear me? I sometimes think that I am talking

to myself because you never give me what I want

or answer me. UGH!!!!!!

Yours truly

DREAM

Life challenges are not supposed to paralyze you, they're supposed to help you discover who you are.

Bernice Johnson Reagon

Dream…..Keep It Moving

You can't have a better tomorrow if you are thinking about yesterday all the time

Searchquotes.com

Has someone important to you ever let you down?

How did you feel?

Have you ever made a promise to someone that

you let down: How did that person feel?

Do you think it is important to follow through with promises? Explain your answer

Extension Activity

Plan your next birthday party. Be creative as possible. Don't forget to include the following:

Theme:

Location:

Date/Time:

Guest List:

Your birthday outfit(s):

Activities at your party:

Extension Activity Cont.

Extension Activity Cont.

Motivation Statement:

When I dream I create vision and without vision I won't grow and If I don't grow I don't move forward and if I don't move forward I don't win!

So I will continue to dream……

Dream

From myself To myself

7 BAD DREAM

My mother came in my room, sat on my bed I

could tell she had been crying

She looked me in my eyes and said Dream I'm

sorry to say that your grandmother is dying

I didn't understand at first I cried out to her

MOM! What do you mean as tears flooded my

face?

She said your grandmother is now preparing to go

to a better place

She has been sick for a while and there is nothing

else that the doctors can do

I screamed find a different doctor one that will

care to make my Nana feel better and make her

new

My mother grabbed me and said Dream calm

down this is all a part of God's plan

She wiped my face and said the doctors have done

all they can

She told me that we have to accept that it is her

time to go

She said that we need to enjoy our time left with

her and let God run the show

I will always remember my Nana for the special

times her and I shared

I will always remember the hugs the kisses just her

showing she cared

I don't know if I will ever understand why people

have to die

I don't know if I will ever understand why God

takes people away knowing we will cry

Rest in heaven Nana she has now earned her

wings to fly

Fly with the rest of God's angels in the sky

Dear God,

Why do you take people to heaven? What is it like there? I love my Nana very much and I wish you would lo let her stay just a little longer. I miss her every day. My mom told me that you are taking care of her but I want her here so I can take care of her. How long will my heart hurt God? Do you hear me? Do you even have an answer for me God? I am waiting to hear from you.

Yours truly

Dream

When someone you love becomes a memory, the

memory becomes your treasure

Lifehack

Dream…..Keep It Moving

The hardest part wasn't losing you it was learning

to live without you

Unknown

Have you have ever lost someone that you were close to? Explain

What are some of the ways you used to cope with losing someone special to you?

Is your family important to you? Explain your answer

Extension Activity

Create a collage using pictures only of things that remind you of the person that you lost.

Extension Activity
Create a collage using only words that remind you of the person that you lost.

With everything I lose I get a bigger gain I will keep it moving

Dream
From myself To myself

8 DREAM BOAT

I have a secret that I have never told

Sometimes it bothers me so bad I feel like I'm

going to fold

I don't know how to tell anyone this is nothing

easy to share

Acting like I'm ok and a smile is getting hard to

wear

Inside I'm screaming help me get rid of this stuff

Inside I'm screaming I need to let it go enough is

enough

Sometimes I wish I could just float away

Hop on a boat and where ever it lands is where I

will stay

If no one knows me then I won't have to explain

all of my tears

If no one knows me then I won't have to explain

the pain from all these years

Maybe I will build my own boat and call it

Dreaming

Leave this life behind and create one with a new

meaning

But then I would have to leave everyone that is

close to me

What am I thinking I can't leave my friends and

family

But how do I get rid of all the pain that I carry

Finding someone to trust is the part that is scary

Everybody always say they will be here for you

Problem is who is just saying that and who is really

true

This is a major secret that is hard for me to let go

I need someone that I can trust, someone that I

really know

My 5th hour teacher told us some things that

happened to her as a kid

Some of the things she shared are the same things

I've hid

I hope she can help me make this secret leave me

be

I hope she can help me clean out the inside and

finally feel free………

Dear God,

I need someone in my life that I can talk to. I need someone that I can trust. I have a teacher that seems like she went through some things like I did but I don't know how to ask her for help. I don't know if she care enough to listen to me or even have time for me. I'm sure she have a family and won't have time to listen to my mess. Can you send someone to me that will listen to me and help me? God are you listening to me? Can you hear me? I will keep talking to you until you answer me.

Yours truly,

Dream

Sometimes memories sneak out of my eyes and
roll down my cheeks

Unknown

Oh yes the past can hurt but you can either run
from it, or learn from it

The Lion King

Sometimes when I say 'I'm Okay' I want someone
to look me in the eyes hug me tight and say 'I
know you're not'

Unknown

What is something that has happened to you that you don't feel like you can talk to anyone about?

How has this secret affected your life?

What do you think you will need to do to get passed your secret and feel free?

Extension Activity

Write a letter to your secret. Describe in detail how you feel about holding onto it and how it has affected your life.

Motivation Statement

I will never give up. What happened to me yesterday no longer matters. Today is a new day to move closer to my dreams

I can do It!

Dream

From myself to myself

9 DREAM CRUSHER

There is one thing that I wished my mom would

have talked to me about

This one thing I would get back without any doubt

This one thing I will never be able to turn around

This one thing I'm trying to shake off but it has

me bound

I had sex

There was a boy that made me feel like I was

important to him

This boy made me feel like he was a basketball and

I was the rim

He needed me

He told me every day I was beautiful and that he

couldn't stop looking at me

He told me that his heart was locked and I was the

only one with the key

He wanted me

We went to his house one day just so happens

there was no one there

He told me he wanted to play a game this game

would show if I really care

He got me

Afterwards I asked myself what did I just do

The most precious jewel I own I gave it to

someone I barely knew

What do I do next I don't even have a clue

I do know one thing that he and I are through

He played me

He got what he wanted and I was no longer his

chick

Everything he said and did was part of one big

trick

I'm ashamed

I know next time to keep my treasure locked in the

chest

This time I'm going to save it for when God sends

me His best……..

Dream!!!!!!!!!!!!

Dear God,

Please forgive me. I never want to disappoint you. I really thought he liked me instead it was all a game. What can I do to make you forgive me? I know I shouldn't of had sex you created me to value myself way more than that. I'm sorry do you forgive me? Do you hear me God I said I'm sorry? I will keep asking you for your forgiveness until you answer me.

Yours truly,

Dream

Never let mistakes define who you are only you
choose who you are and what you become

Unknown

Even Mistakes can get you one step closer

Unknown

Even if you fall on your face you're still moving
forward

Victor Kiam

Have you ever felt pressured to do something?
Explain

What things have you done that you weren't comfortable with? Why did you do them?

What is the importance of waiting to have sex and what is the value of yourself? Explain

Extension Activity

Write a letter to yourself about how much you are worth.

Dear Self:

Extension Activity Cont.

Extension Activity

Instruction: Cut pictures out of magazines that will compare to your worth. Glue/tape them to this page and explain your choices.

Extension Activity Cont.

Motivation Statement

I will not live in yesterday's decisions because I'm wiser today. I will not hold myself in my yesterday because I have decided to live in my today.

I will Keep It moving!

Dream

From myself To myself

10 DREAMED

As I look back over the years of my life I thank

God for the plenty and the few

I thank Him for having had kept me through and

through

As a little girl I talked to Him all the time not really

knowing who He was or His power

As I got older I learned He is my Lord my savior

my mighty strong tower

I know now without Him there would of never

been a me

I know now that He has been there well beyond

what I could ever see

I have been through a lot in my life some food and

it seems more bad

Sometimes were very happy but a lot of the times

were very sad

I don't blame my parents they did the best they

knew how

I just really wish life would have been different for

me up to now

But I have learned to keep it moving and keep my

mind on growing forward

I have learned how to categorize moments of my

past

Pocket the bad memories and make the good ones

last

I stand here today to tell you that not only is your

greater coming it is already here

You are beautifully, fearfully, wonderfully made let

me make sure you are clear

You are a child of God it took me awhile to figure

this out

But I stand here with my testimony to remove all

of your doubt

Stand to your feet and declare it today

Repeat after me and say what I say

I am beautiful I am strong I have a bright future

ahead of me

I will keep it moving and keep dreaming of

everything I will soon be

Look at your neighbor and say if you keep

encouraging me I will keep encouraging you

Together we will succeed and make it through

I bind you from sex, drugs, and pressures from

our peers

I bind you from negativity, depression, and all of

your fears

You have just prayed for your neighbor so God

must honor your request

Keep it moving keep dreaming and let God handle

the rest…………

Dear God,

I have been through a lot in my life. I feel like I need to tell my story to help others. I feel like my story may save others from going through some of the things I went through. God is this what you want me to do? I see so many girls going down the same paths I did. I want to talk to them, I want to help them. God I want to teach them how their test is going to become their testimony too. God do you hear me? God I have talked to you for so many years will you ever answer me?

Yours truly

Dream

You don't have to be great to start, but you have

to start to be great

Unknown

A word of encouragement during a failure is worth

more than an hour of praise after success

Unknown

Success is liking yourself, liking what you do and

liking how you do it

Maya Angelou

The biggest adventure you can take is to live the

life of your dreams

Oprah Winfrey

Have you ever made a decision without thinking it through? What was the decision? What was the outcome?

If Dream were your friend what would you say to encourage her now that you know all about her?

What kinds of things do you say or do to motivate
and encourage your friends?

Now that you know Dream what is your opinion of her?

Do you think that you and Dream could be friends? Explain your answer.

Do you feel like you fit in with your peers? Explain

Do you make others that may not fit in feel welcome to be your friend? Explain

Extension Activity

Create a life map
- Write down your important life events with dates
- Choose pictures from magazines that represent your life events that you chose
- Review your life map in a week, do you need to add more events?

Motivation Statement

Reaching things now I have never thought possible, here I am now I made it here is my life my true dream…….

Unknown

From Myself To Myself

Matthew 7:7

Ask and it will be given seek and you will find;

knock and the door will be opened to you

Dear Dream,

I spoke about you today to my friends. I couldn't stop bragging about how beautiful, wonderful and talented you are. I told them about the last conversation we had and how I was blown away by your wisdom you are smart beyond your years. I remember that last tough situation that you were in but you chose to listen to the whispers in your ears and made all the right choices. I am so proud of you and the person that you have become. I told my friends that I have no doubt in my mind that you are going to succeed beyond success with whatever you want and desire to do. You are a leader and others around you look up to you. Even when you don't know it, you are helping others become better people just by them watching you. Always remember that in the choices you make. By the way I heard every time you called out to me throughout the years. Even when you thought you didn't hear my voice I was showing you the answer to all your questions. Your test has now become your testimony. Run forth my sweet Dream and keep it moving.

Whenever you need me just call me and I will be there. Just between you and me you are my favorite………

I love you to eternity and beyond God……………..

YOU HAVE TO DREAM TO DREAM

Hello Gorgeous,
Thank you for taking this journey with Dream. Now that you have reached the end of Dream's journey it is time for you to create your own. What would that look like? What do you dream about? What and where will you be 5 years from now? 10 years? 20 years? Let's begin to explore your dream big experience. This will require you to use your imagination and go beyond your biggest dreams into your super dreams. I believe in you and I know that you are going to do big and great things. I will be waiting and watching for you.

Love you much
Cynthia Walker

Extension Activity
List 20 good things about yourself.

1.

2.

3.

4.

5.

6.

7.

8.

9.

10.

11.

12.

13.

14.

15.

16.

17.

18.

19.

20.

I CAN DREAM

Write about some of things you have dreamed for yourself.

I CAN DREAM

Give each dream on the prior page a timeline. When will you accomplish that dream.

I WILL DREAM

Why do you think it is important to dream?

I WILL DREAM

Create a vison board. Use magazines, pictures, or printouts to create a poster of your dreams.

I MUST DREAM

How would your dreams be impactful?
To you, to your family, to your peers, to your
community, to your future

I MUST DREAM

Write a letter to the future you

Dear Me:

ABOUT THE AUTHOR

Throughout the journey of this project I was asked the same question by several people 'Am I Dream'? As a young girl I remember being sad a lot. I remember feeling different. I remember feeling like I didn't fit in anywhere. I spent a lot of time by myself in my room playing school with my stuff animals, day dreaming and sometimes just crying. As a teenager I was heavy with a lot of curves. I received a lot of unwanted attention from boys so then I became uncomfortable with my body. I reached a point in my life where I needed to find a hiding place from all my pain, fears, and worries so I became an addict. I began my addiction at the age of 14 but I didn't realize it was an addiction until 36. I was addicted to sex. Sex gave me a high and an escape that helped me forget about my problems for a short period of time. I became a teenage mother at the age of 15 and then

went on to have one at 17 then another at 19.
I am a mother to three beautiful children that
are now adults. I dedicated my life to my
children and forgot about me. I forgot to
dream. Once my children became grown I
began mentoring youth in my community. I
began on a quest to say things to youth that I
always wanted to hear when I was their age. I
began on a quest to make myself available to
youth that needed an ear, a hug, kind words,
encouraging words, or just love. So am I
Dream? I believe some of my life mirrors
Dream's life. What about you what in your life
makes you relatable to Dream? Are you
Dream?

Yours truly,

Cynthia Walker

Coming Soon

This morning though I decided that I
want to start wearing a smile
I want to dress different, think different,
my whole life needs a new style
My life should measure up to the name
that I was given on the day I was born
Instead I always want to introduce
myself first name broken last name torn
I wonder what my life would be like if I
was just born a boy
Instead I walk around miserable and
have to answer to Joy
Hello My Name is Joy (Dream's Mom)